A collection of

Essential English VOCABULARY

Rajesh Sheth
(S. Raja)

The information contained in this book is to the best of the author's knowledge true and correct. The author has made every effort to ensure accuracy of this publication, but cannot be held responsible for any loss or damage arising from any information in this book.

Published in India

First Printing, 2022
Second Revised Printing: 2025

E-book:
Paperback: ISBN : 979-888684871-7 (Notion)

MRP: Rs. 250/-

Gunjan Pablication
Pallavi Towers-1
Navarangpura,
Ahmedabad, India 380009

The woods are lovely, dark and deep,
But I have promises to keep,
And miles to go before I sleep,
And miles to go before I sleep.

- Robert Frost

This Book Belongs to..

A gift from ....

Date: .... Place: ....

This first book is dedicated to...

My lovely parents

And, a lot of thanks to...

My family and friends

Acknowledgement:

As a student of Sainik School Balachadi, I attained a vast knowledge of the English language from my beloved mentors, the **Shri R.S. Rathore, Mr. Mathews, and Mrs. Licy Balaraman** during the years 1970-76. I never knew I was nurtured and trained to teach the future generation.

I owe my gratitude to:

Linda Stanton French, the daughter of a well-known American author and humourist, Will Stanton.

My friend, **Wing Commander, Nilesh Gandhi**.

Mr. Jagdeep Dhebar (JD Sir an author) aka Jasper Dell, for their incessant inspiration to bring about this piece of literary essence under your worthy eyes.

Rajesh Sheth (S. Raja)
Author and Writer/Cambridge English Trainer

Table of Contents

Section 1: Unusual Nouns

Chapter 1:
Nouns always singular!

Chapter 2:
Nouns: Singular and Plural (both)

Chapter 3:
Special forms of words:
Compound words

Section 2: Adjectives

Chapter 1: Positive Adjectives

Chapter 2: Negative Adjectives

Chapter 3:
Range of Variant Adjectives

Chapter 5.
Quantifiers (Determiners)

Appendix:

Rajesh Sheth

Preface

The ever-increasing importance of expected performance (Bands or Points) in the English proficiency tests has insisted and urged me to create and publish this book of **'Essential Vocabulary '**.

An examiner will always look at your range, choice and accuracy of vocabulary, and see how well your words help you express your thoughts.

'Essential Vocabulary' is evaluated in Writing and Speaking Tasks.

These two tasks are productive skills. Developing these skills through 'Essential Vocabulary' is much useful.

To achieve a desired high score, one needs to show a wide range of vocabulary and sentence structure. This concise content of 'Essential Vocabulary ' in this set of three books is thoroughly imagined, compiled, and collected from different, most reliable sources. The content is then corrected, written freshly, and presented in a practical and easy manner for you.

This book, 'Essential Vocabulary ', is only prepared after long face-to-face meetings with inquisitive students. These learners, like you, have always been eager to improvise their Writing Skills by using the immense wealth of 'Essential Vocabulary'.

I have been inspired by my students to present this collection before you. I thank all the students who have followed the footprints of my teachings and guidance.

This revised edition is purposefully created with addition of a few new chapters.

Rajesh Sheth
Ahmedabad

About the Book

This book of **'Essential Vocabulary'** is a must-read for all test takers of the English language.

Lexical knowledge is the knowledge that can be expressed in variable and unique words.

Vast knowledge of vocabulary (Word Power) is nothing but the reference of **'Essential Vocabulary'**. The enhancement of your rich vocabulary through these three books of 'Essential Vocabulary ' shall boost your score. The wider the range of words or expression employed appropriately and suitably, the better the score will be.

This first part of 'Essential Vocabulary ' shall help you reference a variety of words that shall come through your learning process. Word choice is an important task while writing or speaking so that you can impress your examiner or reader or listener. Many words are supported with synonyms and the nearest meanings.

Key features:

- Basic understanding of:
    Collocation
    Less Common Words
    Paraphrasing
    Synonyms
    Connotation
- Abstract nouns with synonyms and the nearest words
- Qualifying words with collocation
- Compound Words
- Adjectives + related Noun
- Variant and thematic range of Adjectives
- Adjectives and their degrees
- Traits (Positive, Negative and Neutral)
- The Royal Order of Adjectives

Rajesh Sheth

Are you taking English Language Test?

We know you are passionate about studying in the UK or the US or Canada. The English Language test is the gateway to these countries.

This information is vital for you while you are taking the The English Language test. To get a good desired score of either 5.5 or 6 or 6.5 or higher in the The English Language, one must achieve all the criteria in a balanced manner.

What are these criteria?

Four criteria are quintessential in any English tests. Out of four criteria, 'Lexical Resource' is one criterion. An examiner assesses the score on a variety of words and idiomatic expressions used, which should be with no repetition. These are meant for Writing and Speaking Tasks.

TAR: Task Achievement and Task Response
CC: Coherence and Cohesion
LR: 'Lexical Resource'
GRA: Grammatical Range and Accuracy

Note: Your faculty will explain you more about these skills.

Remember, this is not a 'Dictionary', but it is a reference book to find out selected words.

Abbreviations:
N = Noun Adj. = Adjective V = Verb Adv. = Adverb

What is Lexical Resource?

A range of vocabulary is focused on in this criterion. A candidate should use a wide range of words and expressions correctly to score high. Using a variety of words and interpretations, one shall get a higher score and shall stand tall in a group. 'Lexical Resource' denotes and includes a few essential factors or prerequisites to fulfill. Now, let's understand a few criteria.

1. Collocation:

Collocation is a way of expression of using two words together that makes a real meaning. It can't be learned by rules. It takes a time of practice for the user to master collocation. One should be aware of the turn of the phrase.

Examples:

Verb + Noun:

Make food/Do work/Commit crime

Adjective + Noun:

Fewer people/Dense forest/Amazing story

Verb + Adverb:

Speak slowly/Run quickly/Write swiftly

Adverb + Adjective:

Quite sure/Reasonably cheap/Seriously injured

Adjective + Preposition:

Nice of/Kind to/Sorry for/Married to

Verb + Preposition:

Speak with/Speak for/Look into/Look for

2. Less common words or terminology.

Using less common words or terminology enhances the quality of the English language. They are either phrases or idiomatic expressions.

Examples:

- Pleasant words can be ***food for thought.***

- I ***can't stand*** his attitude. He is impossible.

- My mother ***runs an extra mile*** to earn money.

- Let's ***go through*** the topic again.

- Police **looked into** the matter keenly.

3. Paraphrasing:

Paraphrase is the interpretation of some words or expressions without changing the meaning. It is used when we want to re-state something with fewer words.

On not finding any word, one must not stop writing or speaking but should use other similar expressions. Usually, synonyms are used to fulfill this criterion.

Examples:

- I need to sit in an ***air-conditioned*** room.

  I need to sit in a cool place.

- They are my ***uncle's children***.

  They are my cousins.

4. Synonyms:

When words are used with similar or nearest meanings they are Synonyms. Synonyms help us choose a wide range of vocabulary.

Examples:

- The word 'Speak' is 'Say'.

- 'Important' can be 'Essential'.

- 'Smart' can be 'Clever'.

- 'Beauty ' can be 'loveliness'.

- 'Ability' can be 'Aptitude'.

5. Connotation:

When any word or expression is rephrased by using another similar expression, we mean it Connotation. It is also important that real meanings or the cultural values are not lost and are presented in a suggestive metaphorical way. It can be referred to as Metaphor as well.

Examples:

- He is **such a dog**. (His behavior is like a dog.)

- He **acts childish**. (It is a foolish act.)

- Teachers are **guiding stars**. (Guides)

- Some people are **bridge builders**. (Connect two ideology)

- Our life is **a roller coaster**. (Ups and downs)

So, work hard and start your journey of Words and Words and Words...

Section 1:

Unusual Nouns

An understanding:

We use some words to identify a person, place, thing, situation, feeling, subject, or an animal. Grammatically, these names are nouns.

Countable and uncountable nouns are the major two types of nouns. A noun that we can count is 'a countable' and one that we can't count but can measure is 'an uncountable' noun.

Say...

- A man: A person (Countable)

- Sheth: A surname (Uncountable)

- Rajesh: Name of a person (Uncountable)

- A City: A place (Countable)

- Bangalore: Name of a city (Uncountable)

- Happiness: Feeling (not a thing) (Uncountable)

- Wood: Material (Uncountable)

- A Mobile: A thing (Countable)

- A Rhinoceros: An animal (Countable)

- Software: An abstract noun (not a thing)

                    (Uncountable)

Chapter 1:
Uncountable Nouns
(Always singular!)

Abstract Nouns :

Points to ponder:

> ➢ These beautiful words are not concrete, but we can feel and experience them. We can't see or touch them.
> ➢ Usually, we need, want, give, take, seek, lose, share and have these abstract nouns..
> ➢ We can derive these words either from Verbs or Adjectives. Example: Speak (V) becomes Speech (N)
> ➢ These words are usually singular but, sometimes, used as plural at places according to usage.

These words (almost 1250) define the...

- Status
- Condition
- Concept
- Idea
- State
- Form
- Stage
- Event
- Circumstance
- Nature

- Behavior
- Feeling
- Emotion
- Sentiment
- Mood
- Situation
- Stage
- Action noun
- Measurement
- Way...

When you use this book, don't copy the words, but understand them and use as per the usage.

Function of
Abstract Nouns:

Abstract nouns are widely positioned in sentence construction when we want to limit the usage of adjectives and verbs. They can replace verbs and adjectives to avoid a repetition of words. A good sentence is always balanced with verbs, adjectives, adverbs and these Abstract Nouns.

Using abstract nouns in a Paraphrase in a test of IELTS:

It is important to understand 'Paraphrase' in task completion of Reading, listening, Speaking and Writing. Paraphrase is the use of other unfamiliar words to convey the same idea.

Questions in tests of listening and reading will have the paraphrased answer. Hence to reach the actual answer, you must know technique of paraphrasing.

A. By Synonyms: Using similar words

- He has ***vast ability to accomplish the task.***
- He has ***immense capability to complete the job given.***

B. By Nominalization: Using a word from the word family

While solving a reading task, you will come through a situation when the question words differ from the words given in the reading portion.

- Text part: Many **people** were too **weak to walk**.
- Question part: **Weakness/lack of strength** of **the citizens** hindered their **mobility**.

The list of Abstract Noun in the following pages contains a few synonyms and some nearest words. You should use these given words wisely!!! A few words are noun & verb both, so they have been identified as (n & v)

A vast collection of 'Abstract Nouns':

1. **Ability**
   - aptitude
   - skill
   - capability
   - capacity
2. **Adolescence**
   - teenage years
   - teens
   - youth
   - puberty
3. **Adoration**
   - love
   - esteem
   - high regard
   - respect
4. **Adventure**
   - escapade
   - jaunt
   - experience
   - quest
5. **Advice**
   - recommendation
   - suggestion
   - guidance
   - opinion
6. **Admiration**
   - value
   - reverence
   - worth
   - esteem
7. **Amazement**
   - astonishment
   - wonder
   - stupefaction
   - surprise

8. **Anger**
   - annoyance
   - irritation
   - fury
   - rage
9. **Annoyance**
   - irritation
   - exasperation
   - vexation
   - indignation
10. **Anxiety**
    - nervousness
    - worry
    - concern
    - unease
11. **Artistry**
    - creativity
    - originality
    - imagination
    - adeptness
12. **Audacity**
    - daring
    - boldness
    - courage
    - cheek
13. **Authority**
    - power
    - jurisdiction
    - dominion
    - dominance
14. **Awe**
    - fearfulness
    - wonderment
    - astonishment
    - dread

15. **Awkwardness**
    o clumsiness
    o ineptness
    o inelegance
    o discomfort
16. **Beauty**
    o loveliness
    o attractiveness
    o prettiness
    o exquisiteness
17. **Belief**
    o faith
    o conviction
    o confidence
    o trust
18. **Benevolence**
    o generosity
    o compassion
    o munificence
    o kindness
19. **Birth**
    o delivery
    o confinement
    o beginning
    o labor
20. **Bravery**
    o courage
    o valor
    o gallantry
    o daring
21. **Brilliance**
    o brightness
    o intensity
    o vividness
    o luster

22. **Brutality**
    o cruelty
    o viciousness
    o violence
    o rough treatment
23. **Calmness**
    o tranquility
    o serenity
    o quietness
    o peace
24. **Catastrophe**
    o disaster
    o calamity
    o upheaval
    o devastation
25. **Chaos**
    o disorder
    o confusion
    o bedlam
    o pandemonium
26. **Charisma**
    o charm
    o captivation
    o appeal
    o magnetism
27. **Charity**
    o help
    o aid
    o offerings
    o donation
28. **Clarity**
    o clearness
    o lucidity
    o simplicity
    o precision

29. **Charm (n & v)**
   - attraction
   - magnetism
   - allure
   - amulet
30. **Coldness**
   - chilliness
   - detachment
   - dispassion
   - frigidity
31. **Comfort (n & v)**
   - ease
   - calmness
   - reassurance
   - relief
32. **Communication**
   - transmission
   - imparting
   - conveying
   - reporting
33. **Compassion**
   - sympathy
   - empathy
   - consideration
   - kindness
34. **Complaint**
   - grievance
   - criticism
   - protest
   - grumble
35. **Confidence**
   - complacence
   - aplomb
   - assurance
   - self-reliance

36. **Consideration**
   - thought
   - deliberation
   - reflection
   - contemplation
37. **Contentment**
   - satisfaction
   - happiness
   - pleasure
   - gratification
38. **Contribution**
   - donation
   - input
   - involvement
   - bequest
39. **Control (n & v)**
   - management
   - dominance
   - authority
   - power
40. **Courage**
   - bravery
   - guts
   - audacity
   - fortitude
41. **Creativity**
   - originality
   - imagination
   - inspiration
   - ingenuity
42. **Crime**
   - offense
   - wrong
   - felony
   - misdeed

43. **Culture (n & v)**
    o civilization
    o society
    o traditions
    o customs
44. **Curiosity**
    o inquisitiveness
    o curiousness
    o nosiness
    o snooping
45. **Danger**
    o hazard
    o risk
    o peril
    o threat
46. **Dare (n & v)**
    o challenge
    o audacity
    o boldness
    o cheek
47. **Darkness**
    o night
    o dusk
    o gloom
    o obscurity
48. **Dawn (n & v)**
    o sunrise
    o beginning
    o commencement
    o daybreak
49. **Death**
    o demise
    o doom
    o loss
    o fatality

50. **Deceit**
    o dishonesty
    o treachery
    o deception
    o deceitfulness
51. **Dedication**
    o devotion
    o commitment
    o enthusiasm
    o keenness
52. **Defeat (n & v)**
    o beat
    o overcome
    o overpower
    o surmount
53. **Defense (n & v)**
    o protection
    o resistance
    o guard
    o security
54. **Definition**
    o delineation
    o depiction
    o distinction
    o explanation
55. **Delight**
    o enjoyment
    o pleasure
    o happiness
    o delectation
56. **Demise**
    o end
    o finish
    o decease
    o doom

57. **Democracy**
- equality
- egalitarianism
- social equality
- republic

58. **Desire (n & v)**
- wish
- want
- longing
- craving

59. **Despair**
- misery
- desolation
- hopelessness
- anguish

60. **Destruction**
- obliteration
- annihilation
- devastation
- demolition

61. **Determination**
- will-power
- fortitude
- grit
- strength of mind

62. **Dexterity**
- deftness
- adroitness
- handiness
- agility

63. **Dictatorship**
- tyranny
- autocracy
- despotism
- totalitarianism

64. **Difference**
- dissimilarity
- disparity
- distinction
- divergence

65. **Dimness**
- softness
- faintness
- gloom
- gloominess

66. **Disappointment**
- dissatisfaction
- displeasure
- distress
- discontent

67. **Disbelief**
- incredulity
- doubt
- distrust
- skepticism

68. **Disparity**
- inequality
- inconsistency
- discrepancy
- gap

69. **Disquiet**
- unrest
- uneasiness
- worry
- anxiety

70. **Distraction**
- bafflement
- disruption
- diversion
- confusion

71. **Distribution**
    - allocation
    - allotment
    - supply
    - sharing
72. **Disturbance**
    - trouble
    - commotion
    - riot
    - uproar
73. **Diversion**
    - distraction
    - change
    - deflection
    - detour
74. **Division**
    - separation
    - splitting up
    - bifurcation
    - partition
75. **Domination**
    - control
    - authority
    - command
    - supremacy
76. **Donation**
    - bequest
    - endowment
    - gift
    - contribution
77. **Dreams (n & v)**
    - vision
    - illusion
    - delusions
    - fancy
78. **Education**
    - teaching
    - learning
    - schooling
    - tutoring
79. **Ego**
    - self-respect
    - self-image
    - pride
    - self-esteem
80. **Elegance**
    - stylishness
    - grace
    - modishness
    - sophistication
81. **Embarrassment**
    - discomfiture
    - awkwardness
    - humiliation
    - mortification
82. **Employment**
    - occupation
    - work
    - labor
    - vocation
83. **Encouragement**
    - support
    - back-up
    - boost-up
    - incentive
84. **Endearment**
    - allurement
    - sweet talk
    - beguilement
    - loving words

85. Endorsement
- backing
- support
- approval
- sanction

86. Endurance
- patience
- stamina
- fortitude
- strength

87. Energy
- power
- force
- vigor
- liveliness

88. Enhancement
- improvement
- augmentation
- development
- enrichment

89. Engagement
- rendezvous
- commitment
- betrothal
- date

90. Enthusiasm
- eagerness
- interest
- keenness
- ardor

91. Envy (n & v)
- jealousy
- greed
- desire
- resentment

92. Evil
- wickedness
- malevolence
- sin
- iniquity

93. Examination
- assessment
- test
- evaluation
- reviewing

94. Excitement
- enthusiasm
- thrill
- elation
- delight

95. Fact
- detail
- reality
- actuality
- authenticity

96. Faculty
- talent
- ability
- power
- aptitude

97. Failure
- breakdown
- stoppage
- malfunction
- collapse

98. Faith
- confidence
- trust
- reliance
- assurance

99. **Faithfulness**
- authenticity
- realism
- closeness
- accuracy

100. **Faithlessness**
- infidelity
- inconstancy
- fickleness
- betrayal

101. **Fascination**
- charm
- attraction
- appeal
- interest

102. **Fatality**
- loss
- casualty
- death
- doom

103. **Favoritism**
- preference
- partiality
- nepotism
- penchant

104. **Fear (n & v)**
- terror
- dread
- horror
- fright

105. **Fitness**
- health
- strength
- robustness
- vigor

106. **Forgiveness**
- amnesty
- clemency
- absolution
- mercy

107. **Fragility**
- weakness
- frailty
- feebleness
- tenderness

108. **Frailty**
- imperfection
- shortcoming
- defenselessness
- ill-health

109. **Freedom**
- liberty
- autonomy
- independence
- liberation

110. **Friendship**
- companionship
- amity
- acquaintance
- comradeship

111. **Generosity**
- kindness
- bigheartedness
- openhandedness
- bounty

112. **Goodness**
- decency
- kindness
- honesty
- integrity

113. **Gossip (n & v)**
- rumor
- hearsay
- tittle-tattle
- scandal

114. **Grace (n & v)**
- elegance
- refinement
- loveliness
- polish

115. **Graciousness**
- courteousness
- politeness
- civility
- sociability

116. **Greatness**
- magnitude
- enormity
- immensity
- vastness

117. **Grief**
- sorrow
- heartache
- anguish
- angst

118. **Guidance**
- leadership
- direction
- supervision
- management

119. **Guts**
- bravery
- courage
- daring
- fortitude

120. **Happiness**
- contentment
- pleasure
- gladness
- cheerfulness

121. **Hate (n & v)**
- abhorrence
- detestation
- hatred
- odium

122. **Hatred**
- extreme dislike
- disgust
- revulsion
- loathing

123. **Hazard**
- danger
- peril
- risk
- vulnerability

124. **Help (n & v)**
- assistance
- lending a hand
- aid
- facilitation

125. **Helpfulness**
- kindness
- neighborliness
- goodwill
- concern

126. **Helplessness**
- defenselessness
- passivity
- blatancy
- vulnerability

127. **Honesty**
- sincerity
- truthfulness
- integrity
- frankness

128. **Honor (n & v)**
- respect
- admiration
- credit
- reputation

129. **Hope (n & v)**
- expectation
- optimism
- anticipation
- wish

130. **Humility**
- humbleness
- modesty
- meekness
- shyness

131. **Humor (n & v)**
- comedy
- wit
- funniness
- the funny side

132. **Hurt (n & v)**
- harm
- injure
- wound
- damage

133. **Idea**
- thought
- design
- plan
- initiative

134. **Idiosyncrasy**
- peculiarity
- eccentricity
- quirk
- habit

135. **Imagination**
- mind's eye
- revelation
- visualization
- thoughts

136. **Impression**
- feeling
- idea
- notion
- thought

137. **Improvement**
- development
- upgrading
- enhancement
- advancement

138. **Infatuation**
- obsession
- craze
- passion
- fascination

139. **Inflation (eco.)**
- price rise
- intensification
- escalation
- augmentation

140. **Information**
- details
- knowledge
- news
- notification

141. **Insanity**
- madness
- lunacy
- psychosis
- mental illness

142. **Integrity**
- honesty
- truth
- truthfulness
- reliability

143. **Intelligence**
- cleverness
- aptitude
- intellect
- astuteness

144. **Invention**
- creation
- discovery
- development
- innovation

145. **Investment**
- asset
- speculation
- savings
- venture

146. **Jealousy**
- envy
- covetousness
- suspicion
- distrust

147. **Joy**
- delight
- happiness
- pleasure
- Joy

148. **Justice**
- fairness
- righteousness
- a fair chance
- coreectness

149. **Kindness**
- compassion
- sympathy
- gentleness
- kindheartedness

150. **Knowledge**
- information
- literacy
- familiarity
- wisdom

151. **Laughter**
- amusement
- hilarity
- mirth
- delight

152. **Law**
- rule
- commandment
- regulation
- decree

153. **Liberty**
- freedom
- independence
- autonomy
- emancipation

154. **Life**
- existence
- biography
- longevity
- verve

155. **Loss**
   - defeat
   - thrashing
   - hammering
   - failure

156. **Love (n & v)**
   - affection
   - adoration
   - worship
   - esteem

157. **Loyalty**
   - faithfulness
   - devotion
   - trustworthiness
   - allegiance

158. **Luck**
   - fortune
   - chance
   - fate
   - destiny

159. **Luxury**
   - lavishness
   - sumptuousness
   - comfort
   - opulence

160. **Management**
   - organization
   - running
   - administration
   - supervision

161. **Maturity**
   - adulthood
   - prime of life
   - middle age
   - mellowness

162. **Memory**
   - reminiscence
   - recollection
   - recall
   - remembrance

163. **Mercy**
   - compassion
   - pity
   - clemency
   - forgiveness

164. **Misery**
   - unhappiness
   - depression
   - gloom
   - sadness

165. **Motivation**
   - inspiration
   - drive
   - stimulus
   - enthusiasm

166. **Movement**
   - progress
   - mobility
   - faction
   - advancement

167. **Music**
   - melody
   - tune
   - harmony
   - composition

168. **Need (n & v)**
   - requirement
   - obligation
   - commitment
   - necessity

169. **Nostalgia**
- homesickness
- reminiscence
- wistfulness
- longing

170. **Omen**
- sign
- portent
- prophecy
- forecast

171. **Opinion**
- view
- estimation
- belief
- judgment

172. **Opportunity**
- chance
- occasion
- opening
- break

173. **Optimism**
- hopefulness
- positiveness
- sanguinity
- confidence

174. **Pain (n & v)**
- ache
- hurt
- soreness
- sting

175. **Panic**
- apprehension
- terror
- anxiety
- horror

176. **Parenthood**
- fatherhood
- motherhood
- fatherliness
- paternity

177. **Patience**
- endurance
- tolerance
- persistence
- fortitude

178. **Patriotism**
- partisanship
- jingoism
- nationalism
- devotion

179. **Peace (n & v)**
- tranquility
- silence
- harmony
- serenity

180. **Peculiarity**
- custom
- oddness
- idiosyncrasy
- oddity

181. **Perseverance**
- insistence
- importance
- firmness
- determination

182. **Pleasure (n & v)**
- enjoyment
- happiness
- delight
- bliss

183. **Poverty**
- scarcity
- shortage
- lack
- paucity

184. **Power (n & v)**
- authority
- control
- influence
- supremacy

185. **Pride**
- satisfaction
- self-importance
- delight
- smugness

186. **Principle**
- code
- standard
- belief
- attitude

187. **Property**
- possessions
- belongings
- goods
- assets

188. **Proficiency**
- skill
- ability
- talent
- expertise

189. **Quality**
- excellence
- superiority
- class
- eminence

190. **Radiance**
- warmth
- glow
- sparkle
- vivacity

191. **Reality**
- realism
- actuality
- authenticity
- truth

192. **Redemption**
- salvation
- deliverance
- emancipation
- escape

193. **Redundancy**
- circumlocution
- diffuseness
- diffusion
- wordiness

194. **Refreshment**
- rejuvenation
- stimulant
- bounce
- energizer

195. **Relaxation**
- recreation
- leisure
- repose
- restfulness

196. **Relief**
- solace
- comfort
- consolation
- cheer

197. Restriction
- limit
- constraint
- restraint
- ceiling

198. Riches
- resources
- treasures
- reserves
- assets

199. Romance (n & v)
- relation
- love
- feel affection
- adore

200. Rumor
- gossip
- chitchat
- tale
- buzz

201. Sadness
- grief
- sorrow
- unhappiness
- misery

202. Sanity
- wisdom
- understanding
- judgment
- good sense

203. Satisfaction
- agreement
- contentment
- fulfillment
- pleasure

204. Self-control
- self-discipline
- discipline
- restraint
- continence

205. Sensitivity
- sympathy
- feeling
- warmth
- compassion

206. Serenity
- tranquility
- quietude
- peacefulness
- calmness

207. Service (n & v)
- examination
- tune-up
- examine
- overhaul

208. Shock (n & v)
- distress
- surprise
- astonishment
- fright

209. Siesta
- rest
- catnap
- forty winks
- midday sleep

210. Silliness
- stupidity
- ridiculousness
- childishness
- madness

211. **Sincerity**
   o genuineness
   o honesty
   o seriousness
   o earnestness

212. **Skill (n & v)**
   o ability
   o cleverness
   o cunning
   o dexterity

213. **Slavery**
   o bondage
   o enslavement
   o servitude
   o servility

214. **Sleep (n & v)**
   o slumber
   o nap
   o snooze
   o doze

215. **Sophistication**
   o style
   o classiness
   o superiority
   o erudition

216. **Sorrow**
   o grief
   o mourning
   o sadness
   o distress

217. **Sparkle (n & v)**
   o shine
   o glitter
   o glisten
   o twinkle

218. **Speculation**
   o conjecture
   o gossip
   o assumption
   o guesswork

219. **Splendor**
   o magnificence
   o finery
   o grandeur
   o majesty

220. **Strength**
   o power
   o might
   o potency
   o muscle

221. **Strictness**
   o severity
   o firmness
   o sternness
   o harshness

222. **Stupidity**
   o foolishness
   o foolhardiness
   o idiocy
   o inanity

223. **Submission**
   o obedience
   o compliance
   o capitulation
   o surrender

224. **Success**
   o achievement
   o accomplishment
   o victory
   o triumph

225. **Support (n & v)**
   o brace
   o buttress
   o mount
   o reinforcement

226. **Surprise (n & v)**
   o revelation
   o disclosure
   o shocker
   o astonishment

227. **Sympathy**
   o understanding
   o compassion
   o kindness
   o consideration

228. **Talent**
   o aptitude
   o flair
   o capacity
   o faculty

229. **Teaching (n & v)**
   o education
   o lessons
   o instruction
   o coaching

230. **Thought**
   o consideration
   o contemplation
   o thinking
   o deliberation

231. **Thrill (n & v)**
   o excitement
   o adventure
   o delight
   o ecstasy

232. **Tiredness**
   o weariness
   o sleepiness
   o fatigue
   o drowsiness

233. **Togetherness**
   o kinship
   o solidarity
   o companionship
   o camaraderie

234. **Tolerance**
   o patience
   o compliance
   o lenience
   o acceptance

235. **Trait**
   o mannerism
   o peculiarity
   o attribute
   o characteristic

236. **Tranquility**
   o Silence
   o Calmness
   o Peace
   o Stillness

237. **Trust (n & v)**
   o faith
   o belief
   o hope
   o conviction

238. **Truth**
   o fact
   o reality
   o certainty
   o accuracy

239. **Uncertainty**
  - doubt
  - indecision
  - hesitation
  - vagueness

240. **Understanding (n & v)**
  - sympathy
  - consideration
  - thought
  - deliberation

241. **Unemployment**
  - joblessness
  - being without a job
  - job loss
  - idleness

242. **Unreality**
  - futility
  - emptiness
  - uselessness
  - pointlessness

243. **Venture (n & v)**
  - adventure
  - enterprise
  - undertaking
  - speculation

244. **Victory**
  - conquest
  - triumph
  - win
  - success

245. **Wariness**
  - caution
  - suspicion
  - circumspection
  - guardedness

246. **Warmth**
  - light heat
  - warmness
  - tenderness
  - compassion

247. **Warmness**
  - heat
  - warmth
  - graciousness
  - reassurance

248. **Weakness**
  - fault
  - weak spot
  - fragility
  - limitation

249. **Wealth**
  - riches
  - prosperity
  - affluence
  - means

250. **Weariness**
  - tiredness
  - exhaustion
  - fatigue
  - lethargy

251. **Work (n & v)**
  - labor
  - employment
  - job
  - vocation

252. **Worry (n & v)**
  - fret
  - be concerned
  - agonize
  - concern

253. **Worship (n & v)**
- o adoration
- o love
- o reverence
- o respect

254. **Wrath**
- o anger
- o rage
- o fury
- o annoyance

255. **Yearning**
- o desire
- o longing
- o yen
- o hunger

256. **Yell (n & v)**
- o scream
- o shriek
- o bellow
- o howl

It becomes easy to use Abstract Nouns as they are uncountable and don't need any article! Isn't it easy?

Can you find a few abstract nouns from this drawing?
This is drawn by my daughter.

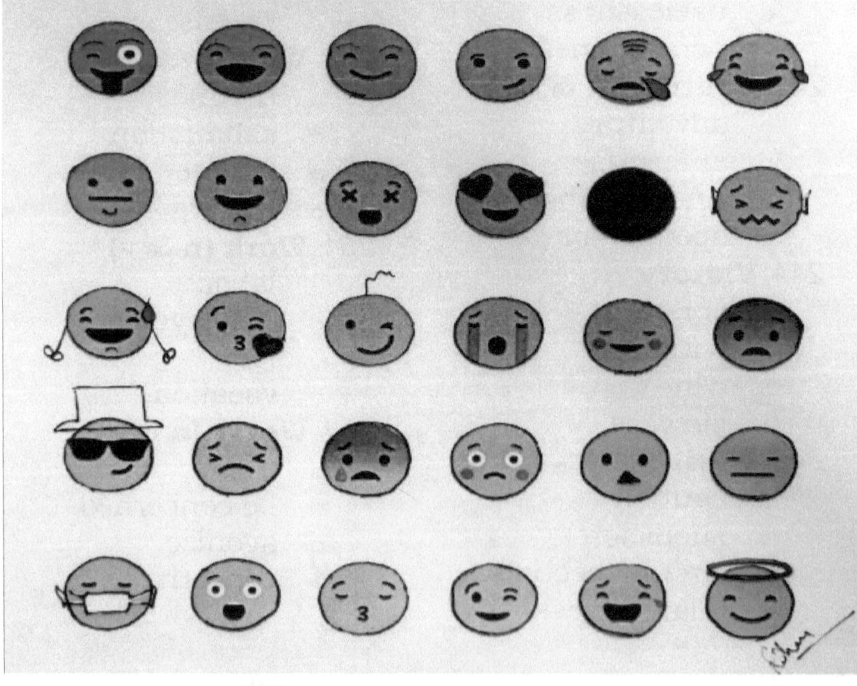

Material Nouns:

An understanding:

Material nouns are either material or natural things. These things are singular and uncountable.

We refer to these words as a mass (a quantity). The quantifiers such as any, some, a little or much are used to show the quantity of material noun

- We need **much oxygen** to live.
- People should use **a little ghee** while cooking.

These material nouns should be coupled with its container, quantity or measurement.

- Please add **a pinch of salt** in the dish.
- **A cup of tea** is enough for breakfast.
- **A full bag of wheat** was donated.
- **A bottle of wine** is nice.
- **A slice of bread**
- **A can of petrol**
- **A spoonful of sugar**
- **A piece of chocolate**

Material nouns include...

- Metals: Gold, Silver...
- Gases: Oxygen, Perfume...
- Powders: Talcum, Chilly...
- Crystals: Sugar, Salt...
- Jelly: Jam, Squash...
- Food: Bread, *Khichdi*...
- Pulp: Mango pulp
- Paste: Mayonnaise, Cheese
- Slurry: Molasses, Mud...
- Liquid: Water, Petrol...
- Grains: Wheat, Rice...
- Fibers: Cotton, Jute...
- Mass: Lava, Snow...
- Dust: Pollution, Smog
- Nuts: Cashew, Almonds
- Beverage: Tea, Coffee...

A few Examples of Material Nouns:

1. Acrylic
2. Alcohol
3. Aluminum
4. Barley
5. Beer
6. Bread
7. Butter
8. Buttermilk
9. Cement
10. Chalk
11. Cheese
12. Chicory
13. Chilly
14. Chocolate
15. Clay
16. Coal
17. Coco
18. Coffee
19. Cotton
20. Cream
21. Curry
22. Diesel
23. Drug
24. Dust
25. Flour
26. Fog
27. *Ghee*
28. Gin
29. Glass
30. Gold
31. Honey
32. Ice
33. Ink
34. Iron
35. Jam
36. Jelly
37. Jute
38. Kerosene
39. Leather
40. Juice
41. Milk
42. Nylon
43. Oil
44. Oxygen
45. Paper
46. Perfume
47. Petrol
48. Plastic
49. Powder
50. Rubber
51. Salt
52. Sand
53. Sauce
54. Scent
55. Silk
56. Silver
57. Snow
58. Soap
59. Soil
60. Soup
61. Squash
62. Steel
63. Sugar
64. Tea
65. Turmeric
66. Water
67. Wheat
68. Whisky
69. Wine
70. Wood
71. Wool
72. Yogurt

Other Miscellaneous Nouns: Things, Observation and Senses

The following examples are always singular and uncountable...And, try to find the nearest words to these to enhance your vocabulary skill.

1. Ambiance
2. Atmosphere
3. Baggage
4. Bonus
5. Climate
6. Clothing
7. Current
8. Cutlery
9. Din
10. Drapery
11. Electricity
12. Equipment
13. Fog
14. Furniture
15. Hair
16. Hearing
17. Homework
18. Housework
19. Incentive
20. Kettle
21. Land
22. Light
23. Lightening
24. Listening
25. Luggage
26. Machinery
27. News
28. Noise
29. Poetry
30. Pollution
31. Rubbish
32. Scene
33. Scenery
34. Sheep
35. Sight
36. Smell
37. Smog
38. Smoke
39. Software
40. Sound
41. Stationery
42. Surf
43. Texture
44. Time
45. Touch
46. Traffic
47. Vista
48. Vision
49. Weather
50. Vision

> Correction Tip:
> - Where is my luggage? (not 'luggages')
> - The furniture in this room is from China. (not 'furnitures')
> - What is the news? (not 'what are the news')

Chapter 2:
Nouns Singular & Plural
Collective Nouns

Please mark the different usage in the UK and the US. Some nouns take plural verbs.

For example:

Government:	The government (they) **want** to pass a new law. (UK)
	The government **wants** to pass a new law. (US)
Staff:	The staff (people) at the new office **are** happy. (UK)
	The staff **is** given new task. (US)
Team:	Our team (players) **work** hard to win the match. (UK)
	That team **works** hard to win the match. (US)
Family:	A family **is** going on a tour.
Audience:	The audience **was** happy in the concert.
Committee:	The committee **approves** the new demand.
	The committee **are** arriving.
Company:	A company **holds** the power.
Firm:	The firm **gets** success.
Police:	The police have come.
	A policeman **is** here.
India:	India **have** won the world Cup.
	India (a team of players) **is** playing the final match.

The following are collective nouns of the group of people/ animals/birds/ things.

Army :   A very big mass of armed forces on land
Band: A group of musicians
Battalion: A group of Regiment
Bench :   A group of jury or Judges
Board: A group of people with managerial powers
Brigade :   A large body of troops
Choir: A group of singers
Class: A group of students studying together
Colony: A group of people having common culture
Convoy: A protecting group (specially ships)
Crew :   A group of people managing ship/airplane
Crowd :   A group of general mass
Fleet: A number of ships under a single command
Flock: A group of animals gathered together
Gang :   A group of thieves or criminals
Herd: Many animals kept under human control
Hive: A collection of bees
Horde: A people or tribe of nomadic life
Library: A collection of books
Mob :   A group of agitated people
Orchestra: A group of musicians (instrument players)
Pack: A group of same kind of animals
Panel: A group of people discussing a public topic
Parliament: The supreme legislative body
Regiment :   A big group of military personal
Shoal: A group of fish
Society: A community having common traditions
Squad :   A small group of military people
Staff: People as employee
Swarm: A group of insects (bees, flies)
Throng: A large crowd
Troop :   A group of soldiers
Troupe: A group of dancers
Commission: A group of persons having some duty
Make some sentences using the words,

The following nouns are always in plural-form but usually stated as singular and sometimes, plural .

1. Alms
2. Amends
3. Annals
4. Archives
5. Arms
6. Arrears
7. Belonging/s
8. Billiards
9. Cave/s (n & v)
10. Chaos
11. Chattel/s
12. Clothes (n & v)
13. Compensation/s
14. Condolences
15. Congratulations
16. Contents
17. Looks
18. Curds
19. Damages
20. Draughts
21. Droppings
22. Drug/s (n & v)
23. Earnings (n & v)
24. Eaves
25. Electronics
26. Environs
27. Fund/s (n & v)
28. Goods
29. Greens
30. Guts
31. Innings
32. Jitters
33. Mathematics
34. Measles
35. Mumps
36. News
37. Nuptials
38. Oats
39. Obsequies
40. Odds
41. Outskirts
42. Pains
43. Physics
44. Possessions
45. Premises
46. Proceeds
47. Regards
48. Resources
49. Respects
50. Riches
51. Rickets
52. Savings
53. Stairs
54. Surroundings
55. Teens
56. Thanks
57. Tidings
58. Troops
59. Valuables
60. Wages

Examples:
- The funds given to this school are not enough.
- Nowadays, teens are very smart.

Other routine items or things are addressed as 'Always plural'.

Garments:
- Bloomers
- Breeches
- Braces
- Flannels
- Jeans
- Pants
- Suspenders
- Braces
- Pantaloons
- Tights
- Flannels
- Pajamas
- Trousers

Tools:
- Bellows
- Binoculars
- Clippers
- Cutters
- Glasses
- Irons
- Pincers
- Pliers
- Scales
- Scissors
- Spectacles
- Tongs
- Tweezers

Examples:

- Can I take these scissors?
- Where are my spectacles?
- These tights are loose!
- Oh you have not worn your pajamas!
- These tights are brand new.

A Note:

Here, we come to a partial conclusion of the chapter of Nouns. The detailed understanding of Nouns is in the book 'Grammar Made Easy' by S. Raja.

Now let us understand Adjectives in the next section. Always remember that you must use at least one adjective (a qualifying word) before a noun. It can be a number, color, quantity or quality, but use it.

Chapter 3: Special forms of Words
Compound Words

Some groups of words are compound nouns. We form them by a combination of two parts of speech. The preceding word acts as a qualifying agent for the successive word.

This usage tells what kind of thing/person/purpose or idea is.

Note: Check Spellings when you write compound words. (One word/Two words/Hyphenated words)

Compound Words:

- **Noun + Noun (Two Words)**

- **Noun + Noun (One word)**

- **Noun + Noun (Hyphenated words)**

- **Noun + Verb**

- **Adverb + Noun**

- **Adjective + Noun (One word)**

- **Adjective + Nouns (Hyphenated)**

- **Verb + Noun**

- **Preposition + Noun**

- **Gerund + Noun**

- **Adjective + Adjective**

- **Other hyphenated words**

- **Perfect participle as adjectives**

- **Other special nouns used as adjectives**

A. Noun + Noun (We Write them Separately)

There is a usage of 'Noun' + 'Noun' combination where the first noun acts as the qualifying word (adjective) for the other noun.

Examples:

Class room:	A room for students who study together.
Country club:	A club set in countryside (rural area
English Class:	A class of students learning English
Table tennis:	A game such as tennis played on a tabletop
Bed room:	A room where bed are placed.
Living room:	A place in the house
English teacher:	A teacher from England or A person who teaches English.
Snake charmer:	One who can charm snakes.
Team mate:	A team member of a team
Concert ticket:	A ticket for a concert

A dining room carpet: A carpet which is in the dining room.

Fish Tank/Garden Vegetables/A washing machine

A frying pan/A wine glass (only glass)

An Indian Writer/A shopping bag (perhaps empty)

Car park/Soap opera

But not:

~~Garage's door~~ but it is a door of the garage or Garage Door

~~My uncle car,~~ but my uncle's car or the car of my uncle

Essential Vocabulary

B. Noun + Noun (We write as one word)

There is one more usage of Noun + Noun, however, these words are written and spelled **as one word.**

Examples:

Countryside/Hairstyle/Lifespan/Lifestyle/Toothbrush

Website/Wildlife/Workforce/Workplace/Toothpaste

Wallpaper/Aircraft/Courthouse/Eggplant/Armpit

Marketplace/Armchair/Cowboy/Mealtime/Bookstall

Nightmare/Eyebrow/Eyelash/Notebook/Rainstorm

Notepad/Oatmeal/Farmyard/Firefighter/Bookstore

Lighthouse/Butterfly/Earthquake/Bookshops...

Note: See the difference in meaning!

A boathouse (A house for boat)

A houseboat (A boat used as house)

C: Noun + Noun (Hyphenated words)

Examples:

- A five-hour journey (We cannot use a five-hours journey)

- A five-hundred note (We cannot use a five-hundred notes)

- A three-month course (We cannot use a three-months course)

- A three-page letter (We cannot use pages)

- Two 13-year-old girls (not 13-years-old girl)

- A half-hour break

- A 2000-rupee note (not 2000-rupees note)

D: Noun + Verb (One and two words)

Hair fall/Rainfall/Sky fall/Toothache/Headache

Moonlit/Home run/Book mark/Root cause

Cloudburst/Bus stop/Earth quake/Foot fall

Snow fall/Jump start/Night wear/Firefly/

E: Prefix/Adverbs + Nouns (Written as one word)

Misuse/Outbreak/Outcome/Outside/Overall

Overcome/Nothing/Backyard/Onlooker/Bystander

Frontrunner/Overage/Underage/Overact/Overarm

Upbeat/Update/Afterbirth/Aftereffect/Aftermath

Afternoon/Beforehand/Background/Backlash

Outdoors/Backyard/Backbencher/Backbiter

Backbone/Backdoor/Afterthought/Crossbones

Download/Upload/Offhand/Upstairs/Outfield

Onstage/Overseas/Underhand/Backdate...

F: Adjective + Noun (Written as one word)

Anybody/Everything/Sometimes/Anyplace/Anyone

Bluebird/Bigfoot/Longboat/Longhorn/ Bigeye (Fish)

Greenhouse/Software/Hardware/Redhead...

G: Adjective + Nouns (Hyphenated)

Good-Looking/Good-Natured/Well-Known

Well-Educated/Well-Paid/Well-Equipped

Bad-Tempered/Ill-Equipped/Hard-Working

Easy-Going/Short-Lived/Short-Tempered

H: Verb + Noun (Can be one or two words)

Bathroom/Rest house/Scare crow/Post office

Post man/Watch man/Guard house/Search engine

Passbook/Showroom/Showcase/Showman/Passport

Payday/Paycheck/Driveway/Drive time/Drivetrain...

I: Preposition + Noun   (Usually one word)

Outlaw/Overcoat/Downhill/Foreplay/Middleman

Afternoon/Offspring/Inbox/Overbridge/Inbound

Inbred/Overpass/Inaccuracy/Inboard/Outbox

Outclass...

(Can be two words or hyphenated)

In-law/In-box/In arms/Out-box...

J: Gerund + Noun (-ing + noun)

Gerund Nouns: Many words with –ing forms are used as adjectives.

Interesting book/Surprising entry/Deafening sound

Embarrassing situation/Confusing idea/Jogging shoes

Disappointing behavior/Running track/Speaking topic

Writing task/Reading skills/Fighting spirit

Parking area/Smoking room/Tiring job/Boring movie

Stunning act/Dancing floor/Dashing personality

Moving story/Mesmerizing moment/Cleaning job...

- Please park your vehicles in the **parking area** only.
  (The area for parking vehicles)

- The **smoking room** is in the next building.
  (Room for smoking)

- Don't stand idle on the **dancing floor.**

- This is **a tiring job.**

- Don't watch that **boring movie.**

- Everybody loves reading **interesting book.**

- Stop that **deafening sound!**

K: Adjective + Adjective

(Usually with hyphen/One word)

Fat-free food/Ice-cold water/Red-hot peppers

Luke-warm water/Long-lived life/Middle-aged man

Absent-minded professor/Endless journey

Kind-hearted man...

Special usage to understand: Endless

(Noun + Adjective) (Adjective + Adjective)

(Verb + Adjective)

L: Other words with hyphen

Note: Compounds which are written with a hyphen.
  Sometimes, hyphen can be removed.

The Make-Up/Well-Being/Twenty-Four/Thirty-Five

Long-Term/Long-Lasting/Full-Scale/Full-Size

Part-Time/Badly Behaved/Fully Qualified

Time-Consuming/Machine-gun/Time Saving

M: Perfect Participles as adjectives

The verbs in perfect participle form are also considered as adjectives.

1. Learned people
2. Decided task
3. Accomplished task
4. Amused child
5. Understood topic
6. Seen movie
7. Fled culprit
8. Sailed boats
9. Injured limbs
10. Torn book
11. Withered crop
12. Shattered dreams
13. Shuttered shops
14. Colored wall
15. Plastered surface
16. Linked paragraphs
17. Nailed plank
18. Anchored ship
19. Departed soul
20. Deported passenger
21. Uprooted trees
22. Agitated crowd
23. Captured memories
24. Sent mail
25. Received message
26. Revised chapters
27. Swapped pages
28. Travelled places
29. Purchased items
30. Discarded items

N: Other Special Adjectives used as Compound nouns or Compound Nouns used as Adjectives!
Remember, all the following groups act as adjectives when they show color, make, ingredient, origin, and purpose.

* Metals, Gems and Stones

* Colors

* Material nouns

* Fruits and Vegetables

* Grains

Examples:

Metals, Gems and Stones:

* I have a **gold chain** worth twenty thousand rupees.
(A chain made up of gold)

* Your **diamond ring** suits on your finger.
(A ring with a diamond on it)

* We should not use **aluminium utensils** for cooking.

* We need a **pearl necklace** for my sister.

* Create some ideas for making a **ruby necklace**.

Colors:

* The lady with the **red necklace** is my wife.

* I love **black current** ice cream.

* **Red wine** is made from grapes.

* We need a **whiteboard** in the classroom.

Section 2: Adjectives

What are Adjectives?

An understanding...

Adjectives play an important role in language. These words show and describe qualities of nouns/ names and give more information.

Adjectives are qualifiers, quantifiers, intensifiers, mitigators and modifiers.

These words define the...

- Quality: An intelligent boy
- Quantity: Many students
- Amount: Ample of love
- Number: Five fingers
- Size: A colossal building
- Shape: An oval table top
- Color: Black stone
- Taste: Sweet mangoes
- Looks: A glamorous girl
- Appearance: Colorful facade
- Origin: An Indian writer
- Age: An ancient art
- Condition: A broken chair
- Situation: A poor bagger
- Make: Wooden furniture

Placement of Adjectives in a sentence:

Adjectives are usually positioned before the adjacent nouns; however, sometimes they are placed after linking verbs as a predicate. One can change the perception as per usage.

Examples:

Adjective before the noun.

1. All the **weak people** are shifted to hospitals.

2. A **developed country** helps the developing one.

3. This is an **accomplished task**.

4. This **dreaded pandemic** has tensed all the people.

5. Bring me some **red flowers.**

Adjective after the linking verb: be, seem, like, feel...

1. All the people who **are weak** are shifted to hospitals.

2. A country which **is developed** helps the developing one.

3. The task **is accomplished**.

4. This pandemic that **is dreaded** has tensed all the people.

5. Bring some flowers which **are red**.

6. He **seems old**.

7. I **feel tired**.

8. He danced **like crazy**.

Intensifiers: (Adverbs)

Intensifiers are used to make adjectives stronger. This intensifies the meanings of words.

Remember that any word that qualifies any adjective is considered as an adverb.

- Your voice is **very sweet**.

- This is **really surprising**.

- I am **extremely happy**.

- This place is **amazingly spectacular**.

- He is **exceptionally good**.

- Your result is **incredibly excellent.**

- He is **particularly punctual**.

- This fact is **remarkably true**.

- He runs **unusually fast**.

- This book is **quite interesting**.

- Your house is **rather old**.

- He can't get a job. He isn't **smart enough**.
  (Enough follows an adjective)

- That movie was **so good that** I watched it thrice.

- I was **too tired** to work yesterday.

- This is **such a lovely** weather.

- I couldn't buy that watch. It was **too expensive**.

- My son is **pretty brainy**.

Formation of adjectives:

These adjectives are usually identified by the suffix such as:

1. **-able/-ible**   understandable, capable, readable, incredible, sensible...
2. **-al/-ial/-ical**   mathematical, functional, influential, chemical...
3. **-ful**   beautiful, bashful, helpful, harmful...
4. **-ic**   artistic, manic, rustic, terrific, drastic...
5. **-ive**   submissive, intuitive, inventive, attractive...
6. **-less**   sleeveless, hopeless, groundless, restless...
7. **-ous**   gorgeous, dangerous, adventurous, fabulous...
8. **-ent/-ant**   important, independent, variant, magnificent...

-an/-ian   human, agrarian, Spartan, veteran, simian

9. **-y**   fancy, hungry, sleepy, angry, balmy, lengthy...
10. **-ish**   childish, selfish, bookish, Spanish, babyish, lavish, feverish

Collocation of adjectives:

What is Collocation of Adjectives?

Collocation is using two parts of speech (grammatical words) – an adjective, and a noun together to give an appropriate meaning, and it should sound natural.

It means a particular adjective should be used to qualify a specific noun.

For example:

- We should say it was **heavy rain,** or **light rain,**

  (Not, **strong rain or mild rain)**

- Doctor replaced an **injured limb with an artificial limb.**

  (Not, **a false or fake limb)**

- The students should wear a **casual dress.**

  (Not, a **common dress)**

- I am afraid of a **dead body.**

  (Not, a deadly body)

This kind of usage in the language is called **collocation.** There is no clear rule but we should be aware of actual usage. Some words just sound right together, while others do not.

In the next pages, we shall discuss a few positive and negative adjectives with appropriate nouns as collocation. The nouns listed in the second column are mostly used with the adjectives in the first column.

Points to Ponder:
Please read and mark carefully, in the next page, that a few
suffixes of words have been marked bold. These suffixes
represent different forms of adjectives.
Isn't it amazing to remember?

Chapter 1: Positive adjectives

A note: The nouns or names in the second column are usually supported by the adjectives given in the first column. Refer to a good dictionary for meanings of these adjectives.

Adjective	Related Noun
1. Accomplish**ed**	task/assignment
2. Adapt**able**	situation/ rules
3. Ador**able**	personality
4. Affectio**nate**	nature/person
5. Agree**able**	idea/notion
6. Alert	person
7. Allur**ing**	personality
8. Ambit**ious**	person
9. Ami**able**	nature/person
10. Amus**ed**	person
11. Attent**ive**	person
12. Bound**less**	bounty/limit
13. Brave	person/heart
14. Breathtak**ing**	scene/scenery
15. Bright	day/future
16. Buoy**ant**	time/person
17. Calm	nature/person
18. Cap**able**	person
19. Charm**ing**	personality
20. Cheer**ful**	nature/person
21. Cheery	nature/person
22. Clever	person
23. Coher**ent**	ideas/thoughts
24. Comfort**able**	place/situation
25. Compl**iant**	student/result
26. Conc**ise**	text/ideas/news
27. Confid**ent**	person/nature
28. Considerate	personality/behavior
29. Consistent	progress/result

Adjective	**Related Noun**
30. Cooperative	person/society/team
31. Costly	affair/thing
32. Courageous	act/person/decision
33. Crazy	behavior/person
34. Credible	act/action/deed
35. Cultured	family/attitude
36. Curious	mind/person
37. Dashing	personality
38. Dazzling	personality
39. Debonair	personality
40. Decisive	point/idea/act
41. Decorous	behavior
42. Delightful	event/thing/place
43. Detailed	information/news
44. Determined	nature/person
45. Diligent	nature/person
46. Discreet	decision/action
47. Dynamic	personality
48. Eager	mind/child
49. Economical	cost/thing/offer
50. Efficient	person/worker
51. Elated	mind/person
52. Eminent	personality
53. Enchanting	place/thing/song
54. Encouraging	attitude/nature
55. Endurable	attitude/task
56. Energetic	person/individual
57. Entertaining	act/scene/person
58. Enthusiastic	person/performance
59. Excellent	result/outcome/
60. Excited	person/being/someone
61. Exclusive	offer/time/proposal
62. Exuberant	person/one/thing
63. Fabulous	offer/place/thing
64. Fair	talk/price/person/decision
65. Faithful	person/animal

Adjective	**Related Noun**
66. Fantastic	idea/place/thing/sight
67. Fearless	person/personality
68. Fine	situation/time/health
69. Frank	opinion/discussion/person
70. Friendly	terms/behavior
71. Funny	act/action/behavior/person
72. Generous	act/person
73. Gentle	person/attitude
74. Gifted	child/person
75. Glorious	moments/time/face
76. Good	person/idea/place
77. Gorgeous	personality/place/scene
78. Happy	moment/person/
79. Harmonious	time/music/behavior
80. Helpful	person/attitude/approach
81. Hilarious	act/moment/story
82. Honorable	person/personality
83. Impartial	decision/choice/verdict
84. Industrious	nature/character/quality
85. Instinctive	quality/skill/trait
86. Intellectual	mind/brain/ person
87. Jolly	nature/person
88. Joyous	moment/time
89. Kind	person/act/nature
90. Kind-hearted	person
91. Knowledgeable	person
92. Likeable	thing/person
93. Lively	person/moment/animal
94. Lovely	person/time/ thing
95. Loving	nature/act/behavior
96. Lucky	person/one
97. Mature	person
98. Modern	time/thing
99. Nice	being/stage/situation
100. Obedient	student/child/one

Adjective	**Related Noun**
101. Painstaking	moment/time/thought
102. Peaceful	situation/time/period
103. Perfect	work/decision/picture
104. Placid	water/place/time/nature
105. Plausible	rate/price/act
106. Pleas**ant**	place/time/character
107. Pleased	personality/moment
108. Pleasing	personality/time/conduct
109. Pleasur**able**	decision/thing/moment
110. Plucky	one/person/character
111. Produc**tive**	idea/ decision/work
112. Protective	person/ situation/thing
113. Proud	person/moment
114. Prudent	individual/act/decision
115. Punctu**al**	person
116. Quiet	moment/time/place
117. Recep**tive**	terms/conditions/ nature
118. Reflective	thought/ideas
119. Reliable	person/company
120. Relieved	situation/person
121. Resolute	attitude/approach
122. Respons**ible**	person/behavior
123. Rhetoric**al**	name/word/idea
124. Right**eous**	values/decision/verdict
125. Roman**tic**	person/situation/place
126. Seda**tive**	drug/medicine/treatment
127. Seemly	situation/thing
128. Selective	attitude/act/behavior
129. Self-assured	person/human being/one
130. Sensitive	person
131. Shrewd	person
132. Sincere	act/action/attitude/person
133. Skilful	act/person
134. Smiling	person/statue/picture
135. Splendid	place/result/outcome/

Adjective	Related Noun
136. Steadfast	decision/act/person
137. Stimulating	idea/thought/time/thing
138. Striving	nature/lecture/person
139. Sturdy	nature/body/physique
140. Successful	person/work
141. Succinct	discussion/conversation
142. Talented	person/personality
143. Tempting	situation/thing/offer
144. Thoughtful	act/person/decision
145. Thrifty	person/attitude
146. Thriving	future/development
147. Tough	situation/time
148. Tranquil	moments/place/time
149. Trustworthy	person/organization
150. Unbiased	decision/verdict/judgment
151. Unlimited	offer/time/food
152. Unusual	situation/offer/position
153. Upbeat	attitude/nature
154. Valiant	soldier/warrior/act
155. Vigorous	exercise/act/work
156. Vital	organs/information/clue
157. Vivacious	temperament/action/one
158. Warm	feelings/approach/weather
159. Watchful	act/action/person
160. Willing	person/nature
161. Wise	person/act/decision
162. Witty	personality/nature/act
163. Wonderful	scene/place/thing/idea
164. Zealous	person/act

Examples:

1. **A willing person** is always successful.
2. Yes, definitely, this is a **wise act.**
3. We are going to have a **thriving future**.
4. That boxer has **sturdy physique**.
5. We like his **pleasing personality**.

Chapter 2: Negative adjectives

Here, are a few negative adjectives with synonyms and possible related nouns. We can make use of a few more nearest related words of negative adjectives. Note that a few adjectives have (N) after the word. It denotes that it can be a neutral adjective as well.

Negative adjectives   **Related Nouns**

1.   **Abrasive**   surface/texture/nature
   - rough
   - coarse
   - harsh
   - rasping
2.   **Abrupt**   idea/sentence/act
   - sudden
   - unpredictable
   - immediate
   - quick
3.   **Abusive**   talk/behavior
   - rude
   - insulting
   - offensive
   - obnoxious
4.   **Afraid**   animal/child
   - frightened
   - scared
   - fearful
   - terrified
5.   **Aloof**   identity/person
   - distant
   - detached
   - unfriendly
   - cold

Negative adjectives	**Related Nouns**

6. **Ambiguous** idea/statement
- vague
- unclear
- uncertain
- confusing

7. **Angry** person/individual
- annoyed
- irritated
- fuming
- irate

8. **Anxious (N)** student/person
- apprehensive
- nervous
- worried
- uneasy

9. **Arrogant** attitude/person
- conceited
- haughty
- egotistical
- bigheaded

10. **Ashamed** person
- embarrassed
- shamefaced
- mortified
- humiliated

11. **Awful** thing/time/situation
- dreadful
- terrible
- appalling
- calamitous

12. **Bad** feeling/time/person
- shocking
- ghastly
- dire
- unpleasant

Negative adjectives	**Related Nouns**

13. Belligerent — person/discussion
- aggressive
- argumentative
- quarrelsome
- confrontational

14. Bewildered — person/situation
- confused
- puzzled
- dazed
- befuddled

15. Boorish — manner/actions
- rude
- ill-mannered
- impolite
- rough

16. Bored — person/talks
- uninterested
- fed up
- listless
- jaded

17. Boring — thing/book/time
- uninteresting
- tedious
- dull
- dreary

18. Callous — person/time/action
- heartless
- unfeeling
- coldhearted
- uncaring

19. Careless — act/attitude/person
- slapdash
- hasty
- casual
- sloppy

Negative adjectives   **Related Nouns**

20. **Clumsy**   idea/situation/time
   - awkward
   - inept
   - ungainly
   - gauche
21. **Combative**   action/attitude
   - argumentative
   - antagonistic
   - aggressive
   - belligerent
22. **Confused**   person/being/situation
   - puzzled
   - perplexed
   - baffled
   - mystified
23. **Cowardly**   act/action/deed
   - gutless
   - spineless
   - weak
   - craven
24. **Crazy** (N)   person/idea/situation
   - wild
   - passionate
   - fanatical
   - extreme
25. **Creepy**   situation/time
   - sinister
   - frightening
   - eerie
   - scary
26. **Cruel**   person/action
   - unkind
   - mean
   - nasty
   - brutal

Negative adjectives	**Related Nouns**

27. Cynical person/activities/tricks
- pessimistic
- mocking
- sarcastic
- distrustful

28. Dangerous deeds/situation/place/person
- unsafe
- hazardous
- risky
- perilous

29. Daunting person/nature/attitude
- intimidating
- off-putting
- discouraging
- scary

30. Deceitful person/deed
- dishonest
- deceiving
- fraudulent
- untrustworthy

31. Defeated team/country
- beaten
- overcome
- conquered
- whitewashed

32. Defective thing/item/article
- faulty
- imperfect
- flawed
- out of order

33. Defiant person/personality
- disobedient
- insolent
- insubordinate
- rebellious

Negative adjectives	**Related Nouns**

34. Depressed person/heart
- miserable
- unhappy
- down in the dumps
- dejected

35. Deranged ideas/task/person
- unbalanced
- unhinged
- disturbed
- mad

36. Disagreeable ideas/suggestions
- unpleasant
- distasteful
- offensive
- nasty

37. Disillusioned person/one
- disenchanted
- disappointed
- disheartened
- cynical

38. Disturbed person/one
- troubled
- bothered
- concerned
- distressed

39. Domineering attitude/person
- bossy
- dominant
- overbearing
- officious

40. Draconian law/rule/commandment
- harsh
- strict
- extreme
- drastic

Negative adjectives	**Related Nouns**

41.   Embarrassed — one/person
- mortified
- humiliated
- gauche
- uncomfortable

42.   Envious — feelings/speech/person
- jealous
- covetous
- green with envy
- resentful

43.   Erratic — attitude/behavior/one
- unpredictable
- inconsistent
- inconsistent
- irregular

44.   Evasive — idea/talk/thoughts
- elusive
- slippery
- shifty
- cagey

45.   Evil — person/soul
- wicked
- malevolent
- sinful
- errant

46.   Faded — thing/item/idea
- gray
- dull
- washed out
- pale

47.   Fanatical — one/attitude/behavior
- obsessive
- dedicated
- fervent
- fixated

Negative adjectives	**Related Noun**

48. Fierce — fight/argument
- violent
- ferocious
- brutal
- severe

49. Filthy — place/area/smell
- grimy
- muddy
- mucky
- grubby

50. Finicky — idea/decision/person
- fastidious
- fussy
- picky
- choosy

51. Flashy — show/idea/appearance
- ostentatious
- showy
- gaudy
- flamboyant

52. Flippant — remark/talk/idea/decision
- frivolous
- offhand
- dismissive
- superficial

53. Foolish — person/act/idea
- stupid
- silly
- idiotic
- unwise

54. Frantic — attitude/person
- worried
- frenzied
- frenetic
- hysterical

Negative adjectives	**Related Nouns**

55. Fretful — person/behavior/act
- worried
- anxious
- fussy
- agitated

56. Frightened — person/animal
- scared
- terrified
- alarmed
- startled

57. Furtive — act/behavior/talk/nature
- secretive
- stealthy
- surreptitious
- sneaky

58. Greedy — person/animal
- gluttonous
- voracious
- hungry
- ravenous

59. Grieving — person/situation/time
- inconsolable
- anguished
- sorrowful
- brokenhearted

60. Grouchy — person/being
- bad-tempered
- complaining
- grumpy
- crabby

61. Gruesome — act/situation/story
- grisly
- ghastly
- horrible
- horrific

Negative adjectives	**Related Nouns**

62. Grumpy person/being
- irritable
- cranky
- cantankerous
- cross

63. Guileful plot/person/idea
- crafty
- dodgy (British)
- crafty
- devious

64. Gullible person/child
- naive
- susceptible
- easy to fool
- innocent

65. Harmful person/object/animal
- damaging
- injurious
- destructive
- detrimental

66. Heavy rain/heart
- weighty
- profound
- weighty
- intense

67. Helpless old man/patient/being
- powerless
- susceptible
- weak
- feeble

68. Hesitant person/nature/decision
- uncertain
- cautious
- tentative
- diffident

Negative adjectives	**Related Nouns**

69. Homeless — person/poor/animal
- vagrant
- dispossessed
- destitute
- down-and-out

70. Horrible — act/movie/story/situation
- horrifying
- awful
- terrible
- nasty

71. Hungry (N) — person/animal/attitude
- starving
- famished
- ravenous
- greedy

72. Hurt — soul/feeling/person
- distress
- upset
- sorrowful
- sad

73. Ignorant — child/person
- unaware
- uninformed
- badly informed
- oblivious

74. Ill — person/animal
- unwell
- qualmish
- poorly
- sick

75. Irresolute — situation/decision/act
- indecisive
- vacillating
- unsure
- hesitant

Negative adjectives	**Related Nouns**

76. **Jealous** — person/nature
- envious
- desirous
- green-eyed
- covetous

77. **Jittery** — person/situation
- nervous
- nervy
- jumpy
- edgy

78. **Lacking** — item/thing/situation
- missing
- absent
- wanting
- deficient

79. **Lazy** — person/one/being
- indolent
- idle
- lethargic
- languid

80. **Lonely** (N) — place/heart/person
- forlorn
- lost
- lonesome
- alone

81. **Malicious** — jealousy/thought/person
- hateful
- spiteful
- malevolent
- mean

82. **Materialistic** — person/attitude
- money-oriented
- worldly
- selfish
- grasping

Negative adjectives	**Related Nouns**

83. Mean nature/attitude/person
- selfish
- self-centered
- egoistic
- spiteful

84. Mysterious (N) situation/place/time
- strange
- unexplained
- inexplicable
- unsolved

85. Naïve person/one
- inexperienced
- immature
- adolescent
- raw

86. Nasty person/behavior
- spiteful
- mean
- malicious
- vicious

87. Naughty person/attitude
- disobedient
- bad
- badly behaved
- wicked

88. Nervous person/being
- anxious
- worried
- edgy
- jumpy

89. Noisy place/thing/situation
- loud
- deafening
- earsplitting
- deafening

Negative adjectives   **Related Nouns**

90. **Obnoxious**   person/situation
   - loathsome
   - hateful
   - horrible
   - insufferable
91. **Outrageous**   Person/act/behavior
   - shameful
   - shocking
   - disgraceful
   - offensive
92. **Panicky**   person/animal
   - frightened
   - scared
   - alarmed
   - fearful
93. **Pathetic**   situation/time/condition
   - wretched
   - dismal
   - sad
   - pitiable
94. **Possessive**   person/attitude
   - jealous
   - domineering
   - controlling
   - scheming
95. **Quarrelsome**   person/nature/attitude
   - argumentative
   - cantankerous
   - difficult
   - irritable
96. **Repulsive**   attitude/act/behavior
   - disgusting
   - revolting
   - nauseating
   - hideous

Negative adjectives	Related Nouns

97. Ruthless — person/nature/attitude
- cruel
- callous
- brutal
- pitiless

98. Sad — person/nature/attitude
- depressing
- gloomy
- cheerless
- miserable

99. Scary — person/nature/attitude
- frightening
- creepy
- chilling
- terrifying

100. Secretive (N) — situation/plot/person
- enigmatic
- mysterious
- reticent
- reserved

101. Selfish — person/attitude
- self-centered
- egotistical
- self-seeking
- self-interested

102. Silly — mistake/act/attitude
- stupid
- ridiculous
- impractical
- childish

103. Slow — act/behavior/decision
- sluggish
- unhurried
- measured
- deliberate

Negative adjectives	**Related Nouns**

104. Sneaky — act/behavior/person
- devious
- sly
- shifty
- underhanded

105. Snobbish — act/behavior/person
- supercilious
- stuck-up
- arrogant
- snooty

106. Sore — result/situation/act
- painful
- stinging
- uncomfortable
- aching

107. Spendthrift — person/behavior/attitude
- wastrel
- squanderer
- compulsive shopper
- fritterer

108. Squeamish — person/behavior/attitude
- easily upset
- prudish
- straitlaced
- fastidious

109. Stingy — person/behavior/attitude
- miserly
- parsimonious
- sparing
- grudging

110. Strange — person/behavior/attitude
- odd
- bizarre
- outlandish
- eccentric

Negative adjectives	**Related Nouns**

111. Sulky — person/behavior/attitude
- morose
- cross
- petulant
- sullen

112. Tacky — person/behavior/attitude
- cheap
- nasty
- low
- tawdry

113. Tense — person/attitude
- stressed
- edgy
- overwrought
- apprehensive

114. Terrible — place/location/attitude
- awful
- dreadful
- very bad
- appalling

115. Testy — person/attitude
- bad-tempered
- irritable
- grumpy
- impatient

116. Thick-skinned — person/attitude
- insensitive
- obtuse
- unconcerned
- impervious

117. Thoughtless — person/attitude
- inconsiderate
- unkind
- uncaring
- insensitive

Negative adjectives	**Related Nouns**

118. Threatening — person/attitude/behavior
- intimidating
- bullying
- menacing
- hostile

119. Tight — Situation/person/attitude
- taut
- stretched
- tense
- stiff

120. Timid — person/animal/nature
- nervous
- shy
- fearful
- timorous

121. Tired (N) — person/animal
- weary
- exhausted
- worn-out
- drained

122. Tiresome — work/situation/job
- annoying
- irritating
- tedious
- wearisome

123. Troubled — situation/person
- bothered
- disturbed
- uneasy
- distressed

124. Truculent — person/attitude/behavior
- hostile
- bad-tempered
- defiant
- argumentative

Negative adjectives	**Related Nouns**

125. Undesirable   work/person/assignment
- unwanted
- unwelcome
- uninvited
- objectionable

126. Unsuitable   work/person/assignment
- inappropriate
- not fitting
- unfitted
- incongruous

127. Unsure   work/situation/duty
- uncertain
- doubtful
- irresolute
- dubious

128. Upset   person/one
- aflutter
- disturbed
- unquiet
- dithery

129. Uptight   person/one
- tense
- anxious
- bothered
- edgy

130. Vague   idea/situation
- indistinct
- unclear
- indistinguishable
- hazy

131. Vengeful   person/one/act
- revengeful
- vindictive
- rancorous
- implacable

Negative adjectives	**Related Nouns**

132. Venomous — animal/weapon/attack
- poisonous
- deadly
- toxic
- lethal

133. Volatile — situation/time/behavior
- unstable
- unpredictable
- explosive
- hot-blooded

134. Voracious — person/animal/attitude
- insatiable
- hungry
- ravenous
- gluttonous

135. Vulgar — comment/talk/behavior
- rude
- offensive
- crude
- improper

136. Wary — person/one/character
- suspicious
- distrustful
- chary
- shy

137. Wasteful — person/one/character
- extravagant
- lavish
- uneconomical
- careless

138. Weak — person/one/character
- frail
- puny
- scrawny
- pathetic

Negative adjectives	**Related Nouns**

139. Weary — person/one/character
- tired out
- sleepy
- exhausted
- worn out

140. Wicked — person/one/character
- evil
- bad
- wrong
- depraved

141. Worried — Person/being/someone
- concerned
- anxious
- apprehensive
- nervous

142. Worthless — thing/person
- of no value
- insignificant
- valueless
- useless

143. Wretched — person/situation
- miserable
- desolate
- heartbroken
- pitiful

144. Expensive — thing/area
- luxurious
- classy
- posh
- exclusive

145. Zany — person/situation
- crazy
- madcap
- screwball
- wacky

A Story of Happiness

Once, a miserable person, Zing, tried to come out of his pathetic life to seek happiness, but he came across many more wretched moments. He tried to seek contentment but; everywhere, he experienced a vague and undesirable situation.

He met a person and thought he was a nice man, as that man gave him some money to spend. But, to his surprise, that man was wacky. He was a crazy person. The currency was counterfeit.

After sometime, on the way, a tired saint approached Zing. The saint had got exhausted and weary after a long walk. He begged Zing to support him with some money to survive. Zing thought that saint to be a miser and thrifty. He was wearing a gold chain around his wrinkled neck.

Having met the man who gave fake money and thrifty saint, Zing concluded that life is zany, desolate and inapt for him. He asked God to call him to heaven. God rejected his appeal.

God asked him to help that saint who was wearing a phony gold chain. Zing was supposed to find more miserable person than him. The god was testing his attitude.

Points to Ponder...

Almost all these adjectives can be converted into Abstract Nouns.

Say: Expensive.....Expensiveness

Tired.....Tiredness

True....Truth

Chapter 3:

Thematic Range of Adjectives
(Variant categories)

This section has a range of variant words that is used as Thematic Range.

- Adjectives of Appearance:

- Adjectives of Condition/Situation:

- Adjectives of Feelings/Situation: (Bad)

- Adjectives of Feelings/Situations: (Good)

- Adjectives of Shapes of things/places/person/ building:

- Adjectives of Size of Building/Thing/Person/ Animal/Space:

- Adjectives of Time: Action/Person/World/ Era/Age/Period

- Adjectives of Taste/Touch/ Look/Texture/ Surface:

Note: These adjectives are with either positive or negative attitude.

Adjectives of Appearance:

Looks or visage of any person/place/scene/picture/ situation/location/thing can be qualified by following Positive and Negative adjectives.

1. Attractive	26. Grotesque
2. Average	27. Handsome
3. Beautiful	28. Homely
4. Blue-eyed	29. Light
5. Bloody	30. Long
6. Blushing	31. Magnificent
7. Bright	32. Misty
8. Clean	33. Motionless
9. Clear	34. Muddy
10. Cloudy	35. Old-fashioned
11. Colorful	36. Plain
12. Crowded	37. Poised
13. Cute	38. Precious
14. Dark	39. Quaint
15. Drab	40. Shiny
16. Distinct	41. Smoggy
17. Dull	42. Sparkling
18. Elegant	43. Spotless
19. Excited	44. Stormy
20. Fancy	45. Strange
21. Filthy	46. Ugly
22. Glamorous	47. Ugliest
23. Gleaming	48. Unsightly
24. Gorgeous	49. Unusual
25. Graceful	50. Wide-eyed

- It looks **fancy.** What an **ugly** thing**!**
- She is **glamorous.**
- The sky is **cloudy.** It is a **stormy** situation, today.
- That bird is nicely poised.
- I don't like to live in a **crowded place.**

Adjectives of Condition/Situation:

State or form of any person/place/scene/picture/situation/location/thing is qualified by following adjectives.

1. Active	29. Impossible
2. Alive	30. Improved
3. Annoying	31. Modern
4. Appalling	32. Mushy
5. Awful	33. Odd
6. Bad	34. Open
7. Beautiful	35. Outstanding
8. Better	36. Passive
9. Breakable	37. Poor
10. Busy	38. Powerful
11. Clumsy	39. Prickly
12. Dead	40. Puzzled
13. Different	41. Real
14. Difficult	42. Recovered
15. Doubtful	43. Rich
16. Drastic	44. Shocking
17. Dreadful	45. Shy
18. Easy	46. Sleepy
19. Enhanced	47. Super
20. Fragile	48. Superior
21. Frail	49. Talented
22. Ghastly	50. Tame
23. Gifted	51. Tender
24. Healthier	52. Terrible
25. Helpful	53. Tough
26. Helpless	54. Wandering
27. Horrible	55. Weird
28. Important	56. Wrong

- This **city** is **alive.**
- This is a **shocking situation.**
- Don't go away from an **important state of affairs.**
- **Modern things** are liked by all.
- These are the **recovered items** from the thief.

Adjectives of Feelings/Situation: (Bad)

Human beings and animals have feelings and emotions. Following negative adjectives express the approach or behavior of a being.

1. Abhorrent
2. Aggravated
3. Agitated
4. Angry
5. Annoyed
6. Anxious
7. Appalling
8. Apprehensive
9. Ashamed
10. Awful
11. Bad
12. Bemused
13. Bewildered
14. Black
15. Blue
16. Bored
17. Bothered
18. Bruised
19. Clumsy
20. Combative
21. Condemned
22. Confused
23. Cranky
24. Crazy
25. Creepy
26. Defeated
27. Defiant
28. Depressed
29. Detestable
30. Discomfited
31. Disconcerted
32. Disgusted
33. Disgusting
34. Dispossessed
35. Distasteful
36. Disturbed
37. Disturbing
38. Dizzy
39. Down
40. Dreadful
41. Dull
42. Egotistical
43. Embarrassed
44. Envious
45. Errant
46. Famished
47. Fanatical
48. Fated
49. Fearful
50. Feeble
51. Fierce
52. Foolish
53. Forlorn
54. Frantic
55. Frightened
56. Green-eyed
57. Grieving
58. Grumpy

59. Haughty		90.	Panicky
60. Helpless		91.	Perturbed
61. Homeless		92.	Poorly
62. Humiliated		93.	Prickly
63. Hungry		94.	Ravenous
64. Hurt		95.	Repugnant
65. Ill		96.	Repulsive
66. Inconsolable		97.	Revolting
67. Inexplicable		98.	Scary
68. Itchy		99.	Selfish
69. Jealous		100.	Shamed
70. Jittery		101.	Sore
71. Languid		102.	Starved
72. Lazy		103.	Starving
73. Livid		104.	Tense
74. Loathsome		105.	Terrible
75. Lonely		106.	Testy
76. Maladroit		107.	Thoughtless
77. Malevolent		108.	Tired
78. Malicious		109.	Troubled
79. Mortified		110.	Uncomfortable
80. Mysterious		111.	Ungainly
81. Mystified		112.	Uninterested
82. Nasty		113.	Unsafe
83. Naughty		114.	Upset
84. Nauseating		115.	Uptight
85. Nervous		116.	Wayward
86. Nutty		117.	Weary
87. Objectionable		118.	Wicked
88. Obnoxious		119.	Worried
89. Outrageous		120.	Zany

- I have a **bad** feeling. He feels **disgusted**
- Don't feel **annoyed.** This situation is **dreadful.**
- It seems **mystified.**

Adjectives of Feelings/Situations: (Good)

***Italic* words are adjectives for nouns.**

- Please keep an *enthusiastic* outlook
- Our **approach is** *amazing.*
- Have a *fabulous* **manner**.
- Their **position is** *high and fair.*
- *Comforting* **thought is** *agreeable.*

1. Accommodating
2. Agreeable
3. Amazing
4. Amused
5. Amusing
6. Appealing
7. Auspicious
8. Benevolent
9. Booming
10. Bouncing
11. Brave
12. Calm
13. Charming
14. Cheerful
15. Chirpy
16. Comfortable
17. Comforted
18. Conquering
19. Contented
20. Cooperative
21. Courageous
22. Delightful
23. Determined
24. Divine
25. Eager
26. Ebullient
27. Effervescent
28. Elated
29. Enchanting
30. Encouraging
31. Energetic
32. Enjoyable
33. Enthralling
34. Enthusiastic
35. Excellent
36. Excited
37. Extraordinary
38. Exuberant
39. Fabulous
40. Fair
41. Fair-haired
42. Faithful
43. Fantastic
44. Fastidious
45. Festive
46. Fine

Adjectives of Feelings/Situations (Good)

47. Friendly	77. Placid
48. Funny	78. Pleasant
49. Gentle	79. Pleased
50. Glorious	80. Pleasing
51. Good	81. Pompous
52. Gratified	82. Proud
53. Great	83. Relaxed
54. Happy	84. Relieved
55. Healthy	85. Satisfying
56. Heartening	86. Side-splitting
57. Helpful	87. Silly
58. Heroic	88. Smiling
59. High-quality	89. Solicitous
60. High-spirited	90. Spirited
61. Hilarious	91. Splendid
62. In good spirits	92. Subservient
63. In the pink	93. Successful
64. Jolly	94. Sympathetic
65. Joyous	95. Thankful
66. Jubilant	96. Thoughtful
67. Kind	97. Tranquil
68. Lively	98. Unwavering
69. Lovely	99. Victorious
70. Lucky	100. Vivacious
71. Magnificent	101. Welcoming
72. Merry	102. Wholehearted
73. Nice	103. Willing
74. Obedient	104. Witty
75. Obliging	105. Wonderful
76. Perfect	106. Zealous

- **A perfect man becomes victorious.**
- **Lucky is the one who is happy.**
- **My friend is nice and zealous.**

Adjectives of Shapes of things/place/ person/ building:

1. Aerodynamic	31. Curly
2. Angular	32. Curved
3. Rounded	33. Curvilinear
4. Arched	34. Curvy
5. Asymmetrical	35. Cylindrical
6. Bent	36. Deformed
7. Bowed	37. Diamond
8. Bow-shaped	38. Disc-shaped
9. Branched	39. Dished
10. Bulbous	40. Domed
11. Chubby	41. Dome-shaped
12. Chunky	42. Fleshy
13. Circle	43. Forked
14. Closed	44. Furrowed
15. Coiled	45. Heart-shaped
16. Concave	46. Hexagonal
17. Concentric	47. Hollow
18. Congruent	48. Hunched
19. Conical	49. In a circle
20. Contorted	50. Jagged
21. Contoured	51. Kite-shaped
22. Convex	52. Notched
23. Convoluted	53. Oblong
24. Corpulent	54. Octagonal
25. Corrugated	55. Octahedral
26. Creased	56. Outsized
27. Crooked	57. Oval
28. Crystalline	58. Parallel
29. Cubical	59. Peewee
30. Cuboids	60. Pentagonal

Adjectives of Shapes of things/places/person/building

61. Perpendicular
62. Piercing
63. Pleated
64. Plumb
65. Pointed
66. Pointy
67. Pyramidal
68. Quadrilateral
69. Rangy
70. Rectangular
71. Reshaped
72. Ribbed
73. Rippled
74. Round
75. Ruffled
76. Saw-like
77. Scrawny
78. Semi circle
79. Serrated
80. Sharp
81. Spherical
82. Spiral
83. Square
84. Star-shaped
85. Steep
86. Stooped
87. Stout
88. Straight
89. Symmetrical
90. Tapered
91. Three Dimensional
92. Triangular
93. Tucked
94. Twisted
95. Two Dimensional
96. Undersized

Examples:

- **An arched passage** always welcomes me.
- **This zigzag road** goes to market.
- **These serrated teeth** are dangerous.
- Sugar is **crystalline shaped.**
- **A stooped man** is very old.
- A **semi circle** is always half of the **circle.**
- **Chubby cheeks** are pulled by all.
- I have an **oval shaped dining table** which has **twisted legs of wood.**

Adjectives of Size of Building/Thing/Person/Animal/Space:

1.	Big	34.	Minor
2.	Bony	35.	Minuscule
3.	Bottomless	36.	Narrow
4.	Broad	37.	Obese
5.	Bulky	38.	Overweight
6.	Colossal	39.	Petite
7.	Corpulent	40.	Plane
8.	Deep	41.	Plump
9.	Diminutive	42.	Pocket-sized
10.	Dumpy	43.	Puny
11.	Elfin	44.	Scrawny
12.	Emaciated	45.	Shallow
13.	Enormous	46.	Short
14.	Epic	47.	Skeletal
15.	Fat	48.	Skinny
16.	Gargantuan	49.	Slender
17.	Giant	50.	Small
18.	Gigantic	51.	Soaring
19.	Grand	52.	Spacious
20.	Great	53.	Squat
21.	Heavy	54.	Stout
22.	Hefty	55.	Substantial
23.	High	56.	Tall
24.	Huge	57.	Teensy
25.	Immense	58.	Teeny
26.	Jumbo	59.	Teeny-Tiny
27.	Large	60.	Thin
28.	Lean	61.	Tiny
29.	Little	62.	Undersized
30.	Low	63.	Unfathomable
31.	Mammoth	64.	Vast
32.	Massive	65.	Whooping
33.	Miniature	66.	Wide

Adjectives of Time:
Action/Person/World/Era/Age/Period
(Adv = Adverb   Pre. = Preposition)

1. Abrupt
2. Abundant
3. Accurate
4. Adult
5. Aged
6. Ago
7. Ahead (Adv.)
8. Ancient
9. Antiquated
10. Antique
11. Archaic
12. Bad
13. Behind (Adv.)
14. Breathtaking
15. Brief
16. Brisk
17. Childish
18. Closing
19. Contemporary
20. Creative
21. Current
22. Deceased
23. Delayed
24. Early (Adv.)
25. Enough
26. Epic
27. Epigrammatic
28. Existing
29. Extended
30. Extensive
31. Fabulous
32. Fast (Adv)
33. Fleeing
34. Flourishing
35. Future
36. Good
37. Grown-up
38. Hasty
39. Hurried
40. Immediate
41. Infant
42. Last (Adv.)
43. Late (Adv.)
44. Latest
45. Limited
46. Little
47. Local
48. Long (Adv.)
49. Long-ago
50. Modern
51. Modern-day
52. More (Adv.)
53. Much (Adv.)
54. Nippy
55. Old
56. Old-Fashioned
57. On hand
58. On the dot
59. Opening
60. Out-dated
61. Past (Pre)
62. Pending
63. Plenty of
64. Postponed
65. Preceding
66. Prehistoric

Adjectives of Time: Action/Person/World/Era/Age/Period

67. Premature
68. Present
69. Previous
70. Primal
71. Primitive
72. Primordial
73. Prompt
74. Prosperous
75. Punctual
76. Quick
77. Rapid
78. Ripened
79. Scanty
80. Scarce
81. Seasoned
82. Short
83. Short-lived
84. Slow
85. Sluggish
86. Spare
87. Speedy
88. Splendid
89. Squat
90. Standard
91. Succinct
92. Sudden
93. Swift
94. Traditional
95. Unhurried
96. Upcoming
97. Veteran
98. Weathered
99. Wonderful
100. Young
101. Youthful

Some Examples:

1. In this modern era, we have become technocrats.
2. We can't catch fleeing time.
3. A little time is left to save the natural resources.
4. Antique things are worthy.
5. A succinct episode is always inspiring.

A note: Readers should use these adjectives with related nouns so that Collocation is justified. Rather than memorizing these words, seeking advice from your mentor is must.

Adjectives of Taste/Touch/ Look/ Texture/Surface:

Many items such as food, liquids, crystals, vapor, fumes, smoke, and other things are defined by these adjectives.

1.	Acidic	29.	Dirty
2.	Appetizing	30.	Dry
3.	Aromatic	31.	Dusty
4.	Artificial	32.	Edible
5.	Bitter	33.	Fatty
6.	Blended	34.	Filthy
7.	Blistering	35.	Flaky
8.	Boiling	36.	Flavorful
9.	Brackish	37.	Fluffy
10.	Brawny	38.	Foamy
11.	Breezy	39.	Freezing
12.	Broken	40.	Fried
13.	Bubbly	41.	Frothy
14.	Bumpy	42.	Frozen
15.	Chilly	43.	Fusty
16.	Cold	44.	Fuzzy
17.	Colored	45.	Glittering
18.	Cool	46.	Glossy
19.	Creamy	47.	Glutinous
20.	Creepy	48.	Gooey
21.	Crooked	49.	Greasy
22.	Cuddly	50.	Grubby
23.	Curly	51.	Gummy
24.	Damaged	52.	Hard
25.	Damp	53.	Hot
26.	Decayed	54.	Icy
27.	Delectable	55.	Insipid
28.	Delicious	56.	Invigorating

Adjectives of Taste/Touch/Look/Texture/Surface

57.	Juicy	88.	Scented
58.	Loose	89.	Scrumptious
59.	Luscious	90.	Searing
60.	Melted	91.	Seasoned
61.	Mouth watering	92.	Shaggy
62.	Muddy	93.	Shaky
63.	Nebulous	94.	Sharp
64.	Non-organic	95.	Shining
65.	Nourishing	96.	Shivering
66.	Nutritious	97.	Silky
67.	Oily	98.	Sizzling
68.	Opaque	99.	Sleek
69.	Organic	100.	Slimy
70.	Palatable	101.	Slippery
71.	Peppery	102.	Smeared
72.	Perfumed	103.	Smooth
73.	Piquant	104.	Soft
74.	Plastic	105.	Soiled
75.	Prickly	106.	Solid
76.	Pungent	107.	Soothe
77.	Rainy	108.	Sour
78.	Razor-sharp	109.	Spicy
79.	Ripe	110.	Squashy
80.	Roasted	111.	Stale
81.	Roasting	112.	Steady
82.	Rotten	113.	Sticky
83.	Rough	114.	Stimulating
84.	Saline	115.	Strong
85.	Salty	116.	Succulent
86.	Savory	117.	Sugary
87.	Scattered	118.	Sultry

119.	Sweet	131.	Warm
120.	Synthetic	132.	Weak
121.	Tangy	133.	Wet
122.	Tarnished	134.	Wooden
123.	Tart	135.	Yummy
124.	Tasteless	136.	Zesty
125.	Tasty		
126.	Tender		
127.	Tight		
128.	Transparent		
129.	Uneven		
130.	Viscous		

Some examples:

1. Some food items are **very spicy.**
2. This sweet dish is **yummy.**
3. **Stale food** should not be consumed.
4. We avoid consuming **oily food**.
5. **Sugary** food is liked by children.
6. The surface of this table is **uneven but smooth.**
7. We may slip on **slippery surfaces**.
8. The **bumpy roads** make me sick.
9. This **shining surface** is liked by all.
10. I walked on the **rough road.**

An assignment:

Choose the best qualitative words (adjectives) for Pizza, Tomato Soup, Burger, Cake, Butter and Cheese.

Can you pick out all the adjectives of food items that you eat or like? When you do this, make a paragraph about food dishes that you like the most.

1.   I love .... pizza. Its taste is ...., ..., and .... When it comes out of the oven it is very .... and .... But, My sister loves .... and .... pizza.

2.   I love eating .... chocolate. My chocolate bar should be ...., ..., and .... Whenever I consume chocolate bar, I be ....

3.   Early in the morning, my mother asks me to drink a glass of .... and .... milk. For me milk is very .... and .... According to doctors, any milk which is .... and .... , it is .... for health.

4.   Tomato soup is .... for our health. We should choose .... and .... tomatoes for boiling. Its color is .... When I go to any restaurant, I order .... and .... tomato soup.

5.   On every birthday we love cutting .... cakes. These cakes are very .... My choice of mine is a .... and .... cake. It contains .... cheery on the top. It is ....in color and the taste is.................. and ....

How are Adverbs formed from Adjectives?

By process of transformation adverbs are usually formed by adding -ly after an adjective.

- Slow   Slowly
- Prompt   Promptly
- Brief   Briefly
- Quick   Quickly
- Perfect   Perfectly
- Careful   Carefully
- Serious   Seriously
- Heavy   Heavily

But not....

- Fast to fastly...it is fast to fast..
- Hard to hardly...it is hard to hard (Hardly = scarcely)
- Good to goodly...it is good to well
- Late to lately...it is late to late (Lately = recently)

Examples:

- He is a **quick runner**. He **runs quickly.**
- Please be **quiet**. Please **speak quietly.**
- My brother is a **careful driver**. My brother **drives carefully.**
- You speak **perfect English**. You **speak** English **perfectly.**
- Lets do some **hard work**. We should **work hard.**
- This is a **fast train**. It **runs fast.**

Note:
**We will discuss more about Adverbs in the book
Essential Vocabulary part 2.**

Chapter 5. Quantifiers

Quantifiers (Determiners) define and show Quantity/ Volume/Amount/Number/Weight/Portion of nouns. While construction of any sentence, using the nouns which are countable or uncountable, we use one of these words.

Almost all determiners are classified among Adjectives.

Determiners:

1. A few
2. A bit of
3. A great deal of
4. A large number of
5. A little
6. A lot of
7. A pinch of
8. A quantity of
9. A small number of
10. A vast number of
11. Abundant
12. Additional
13. Adequate
14. All
15. Ample of
16. Any
17. As much as
18. Blank
19. Bountiful
20. Bulk
21. Copious
22. Countable
23. Countless
24. Each
25. Either
26. Empty
27. Enough
28. Every
29. Excess
30. Extra
31. Fathomable
32. Few
33. Generous
34. Handful
35. Hardly any
36. Heavy
37. Hefty
38. Immeasurable
39. Incalculable
40. Inestimable
41. Infinite
42. Innumerable
43. Large amount of
44. Left over
45. Light
46. Lion's share
47. Loads of
48. Lots of
49. Major
50. Majority
51. Many
52. Mouthful

53. Much	68. Spare
54. Neither	69. Surplus
55. Numerous	70. Substantial
56. Overabundance	71. Sufficient
57. Part of	72. Superfluity
58. Plenty	73. Superfluous
59. Plentiful	74. Tremendous
60. Plethora of	75. Uncountable
61. Profound	76. Unfathomable
62. Profuse	77. Unstated
63. Robust	78. Various
64. Scanty	79. Vast amount of
65. Several	80. Very less
66. Sizeable	81. Weighty
67. Some	

Examples:
- There is **hardly** any water in this tank to use.
- **Various** English books are written by S. Raja.
- We need **substantial** amount of food to survive.
- The earth has **unstated** amount of natural resources.
- There is **plethora of** arguments from the opposition.

Remember, these quantifiers are for both countable, and uncountable types of nouns. Try to imagine the thing/ people/ any object/ place after it and write in the notebook. Speak aloud to practice.

- **Uncountable Nouns: Any/A little/Some/ Much/Plenty...**
- **Countable Singular Nouns: Any/Each/Either...**
- **Plural Nouns: A few/Many/ Some/Several/Various**

**The detailed understanding of countable and uncountable nouns is in the book
'The Grammar Made Easy' by S. Raja.**

A few examples to revise the learning :

- **A** child gets **immense great happiness** when it meets mother.
- My **great country** has given **many brawny warriors**.
- A glass of **clean, cold water** quenches the thirst of a **thirsty traveller.**
- I have **a beautiful small red bicycle.**
- **Many intelligent students** clear their **tough examinations** with the support of **a great number of unusual words** that come in English language.
- Columbus was a **adventurous and curious sailor** who travelled through **unfathomable vast oceans.**

A note from the author:

Till now, we have covered almost all the important and casual usages of adjectives. Having learnt these adjectives, we should not forget using at least one adjective or a determiner prior to any noun: an abstract noun or a material noun. Even common nouns and collective nouns should be qualified with these adjectives.

Appendix:

A few Common Idiomatic Expressions & Their Meanings

1. My brother was **tickled pink** by the good news that he never expected. (To be very happy)
2. Your team was **hands down** the best team in the city. (Without competition)
3. I don't know the reason but she's been feeling pretty **down in the dumps** for a few days. (Sad or depressed)
4. The season is very bad. I'm feeling **sick as a dog**! (To be sick)
5. It seems that you are **under the weather**. Take rest. (Unwell)
6. Hey, You, **Rise and shine**! The day in over yet. (To be happy!)
7. The competition was quite tough. It was **close, but no cigar**. (Away from winning)
8. We are far from the city. We have to wait **till the cows come home**. (For a very long time)
9. Wow! This monsoon, it's raining **cats and dogs** out there! Let's enjoy it. (Very hard rain)
10. That incessant irritating sound is **driving me up the wall**! (To make annoyed)
11. This new assignment is **a piece of cake**. (Very easy)
12. Despite his rule breaking, he was only given **a slap on the wrist**. (A mild punishment)
13. Oh! This branded T-shirt costs **an arm and a leg**. (Extremely expensive)
14. No, Don't get enraged. I was just **pulling your leg**. (Making a joke)
15. This logic is confusing. **It's Greek** to me! (Cannot understand)
16. This is not the final test. **Keep** your **chin up**. (Be happy)

A few Common Idiomatic Expressions & Their Meanings

17. You have a lot of time to complete the work. **Hold your horses**. (Be patient)
18. Don't worry. You are not alone, we're all i**n the same boat**. (In the same position)
19. The monsoon is here. But heavy rain is a bit of **a loose cannon**. (Unpredictable)
20. He is a lazy boy. He's going to clean his room **when pigs fly**. (Impossible/ never)
21. He **turned a deaf ear** to my advice so he failed the test. (To disregard)
22. We are going to win this match **by hook or by crook** (By any means)
23. Whenever misbehavior is concerned I **put my foot down.** (To take a resolute stand)
24. Radhika has **made up her mind** to study in Canada.(Decided)
25. Remember, your steady work is sure to be rewarded **in the long run.** (Ultimately)
26. Mother saved her child from fire **in the nick of time**. (Just at the right moment)
27. The Covid 19 pandemic seems to have got quite **our of hand.** (Beyond control)
28. You should **hit the nail on the head** when you get a chance to solve the Problem. (to act the right thing)
29. The young rider, without a licence, **took to his heels** on seeing a policeman. (Ran off)
30. I visit my distant friend's home **once in a blue moon**.(Rarely)
31. **Out of the blue,** my class teacher asked a random question. (Unexpectedly, suddenly)
32. My mother **has green fingers.** You must see her flourishing kitchen Garden. (Expert at gardening)

A few Common Idiomatic Expressions & Their Meanings

33. Raju was in **seventh heaven** when he published his first book. (Very happy)
34. The peon was **caught red handed** when he was about to open the principal's locker.
     (Caught doing a wrong act)
35. Stop preparing for the exam **at the eleventh hour.** It will not fetch good results.
     (At the last moment)
36. Parth decided **to burn the midnight oil** to clear the SAT exam. (To put in a lot of effort)
37. He was jailed for ten years. Later he **turned over a new leaf** and became a good citizen.
     (A complete change for the betterment)
38. He is such a horny man! He **blows his trumpet** loud. (Boasting his work)
39. He is caught. Now he has **got into the hot water**. (get in trouble)
40. He didn't fight fair. He **hit below the belt.** (Unfair act)
41. The judgement will be fair enough. Every judge **sits on the fence.** (Always unbiased)
42. During the entire family discussion I was supposed **to hold my tongue.** (Keep quite)
43. In the last five minutes our team **turned the tables** and we won the match. (Reverse the result)
44. Some people **keep the pot boiling on**. They never want any positive result. (Continue the discussion)
45. This chap is born with a silver spoon. He has all the happiness of the world.
     (Born in a very rich family)

Praises:

Linda Stanton French (USA) says: *'You have a good command of the rules of English. These books are edited carefully. I hope this book is a success.'*

Sakshi Shah (A student of B.Com.) says: *'The first impression of this book to me was something like : All in one. Yes, it is useful for everyone. Everything can be found in this book, that is something really unique about it. I do find it perfect not only for test takers but also for people who are learning this language.*

Mukesh Raval (An educator) says: *'Sheth Sir has been teaching English for many years in my academy. His expertise in the language, and the way of teaching have influenced hundred of students. This book of Essential Vocabulary shall be the best tool for all the students.'*

Meshwa Soni (A First Year college student) says: *' I am a student of Sheth Sir since 2018. His creative notes have helped me a lot. Having gone through this book, I am so delighted that this shall help me in enhancing my vocabulary. The collection and compilation are awesome. I have never found a book like this.*

Ferin Patel (Std. 11) says: *'This book is a unique jewel of a kind. The content, the usefulness, and the outcome, all are very useful for a student like me. I have gathered a lot of knowledge of word power from this book. This is a successful publication.'*

Prof. NK Dave (An author of Commerce books) says: *' This book seems to be a result of hard work. Rajesh has taken much toil and trouble to support his students. This book shall allow the learners of English language in mastering new words.*

Nilesh Gandhi (A veteran Airforce officer) says: *'Firstly my congratulations to you for this mammoth task that you have undertaken ! I became a student again & definitely brushed up my language skills.*

Essential Vocabulary